Simple Thoughts

By

Ġorġ Peresso

Introduction By
Prof. Charles Briffa

Edited by
Walter Joseph Schenck, Jr.

Simple Thoughts
Copyright © 2018
by Ġorġ Peresso

ISBN-13:978-0936978055 (Pheasant Run Publications)
ISBN-10:0936978058

Pheasant Run Publications
Jacksonville, FL 32258

Cover: Horizons-MALTA
Ceramic sculpture 'PEACE' by: Godfrey Xuereb

Printed in the United States of America

Thank You

Annette Apap,
Prof. Charles Briffa,
Elisabeth Fenech,
Horizons-Malta,
Irene Mangion,
Ylenia Peresso,
Louise Rickman,
Godfrey Xuereb,
Lydia Zammit,
Reuben Pace.

Contents

Contents, Con't.

Dedication

To
Walter and Molly Schenck

And

To my sister,
Myriam Peresso

৯৹৵৹৵৹৵

Though they did not inspire these poems,
They conspired to have them published.

Biography

ĠORĠ (George) PERESSO is a Maltese writer, poet and broadcaster, born in 1939, at Vittoriosa (Il-Birgu), the first city of the Knights of Malta on the Mediterranean Islands.

Ġorġ wrote several novels, one of which, *Ir-Raġel ta' Wħdu - The Solitary Man)* received second place in the National Book Awards, (2012). His first novel, *Ħajja ta' kelb - A Dog's Life,* was given a Special Prize by the National Prize Awards Committee for its orginal style, (2001). His collection of short stories, *Imħabba Buffa— Love is a Clown, 2008,* contains very short-short stories of three hundred words each). His childhood autobiography (*It-Tifel tan-Nanna - The Grandmother's Son,* 2009) was also placed second in the same National Book Awards. Ġorġ published two books of poetry, *(Għażilt li nħobb—I chose Love, 1987,* and *Kieku Alla kellu n-nervi—If God had a bad temper,* a collection of neive poems,) co-authored a book of poetry (*Alfa,*) with Rena Balzan, Charles Caruana and Salv Sammut, winner of second place in the 2000 edition of the NBA. Published two books of poetry in Italian, *Silenzi per una notte—Silences for a night, 1998,* and *I colori del mio Silenzio—The Colors of my Silence.)* Most of his books were originally scripted for radio and television programmes. His latest novel, *Vjola l-kulur tal-Imħabba - Purple is the colour of Love (2017)* is satirical novel on socio-political issues.

Winner of eight prizes by the Malta Broadcasting Authority for radio programmes, including documentaries, (*Rimja - Shoots; Ruma fis-sena Mqaddsa—Rome in the Holy Year; Dan x'Ċiċerun hu! — What kind of Cicero is this!; Dab x'annimal hu!—What kind of animal is this; Abjad u Iswed—White and Black; Jien, Waħdi Intom u Jien—Alone, You, and I;* and two radio-plays *Il-Maqdes ta' Fuq u l-Maqdes ta' Isfel - The Two neolithic Temples; Jum fil-Ħajja ta' Nathalie Peltier—A day in the Life of Nathalie Peltier.)*

He is still active as a writer, lecturer, translator, and broadcaster.

Paraphrasing G.K. Chesterton, for me a poet is an absentminded man with the presence of mind somewhere else. Around him and far away. Inside him and outside himself. Challenged and challenging. These poems are the result of this attitude, fragments of thoughts and observation, bewilderment and anger, happiness and sadness. Hence, no poem is complete. Each poem is simply fragments of thoughts that turn each man into a poet. Because even readers of poetry are poets.

"The aesthetic surface of Peresso's poems is rather smooth and clear, since rhythm, language, and lineation all work in combination for the general effect."

- Prof. Charles Briffa.

Introduction

Simple Thoughts in an Intellectual Climate
By
Charles Briffa

Introduction

The concept of *Simple Thoughts* implies mainly that Ġorġ Peresso's poetry is accessible to the average reader, but at the same time it also suggests that it is thought-provoking for the attentive reader. It combines serious comments with certain techniques showing the way Peresso thinks. My investigation here rests not only on the strategies he uses in these poems (which are representative of his literature as a whole) but it relies also on the fact that he is a friend whom I consider to be an existential thinker who sets up his own ethical reality.

Peresso studied literature, philosophy, and theology. He lectured on media subjects and pastoral theology but his main occupation in life was broadcasting. Before he retired he was head of cultural programs for television and a creative director of television and radio programs. He also wrote and produced drama and documentaries for local radio and television stations. Apart from poetry he wrote and published a novel, *Ħajja ta' Kelb* (1999—A Dog's Life) and, what he calls, a docu-drama, *Il-Mara ta' Dlielha Twil* (2014—The Woman with Long Flowing Hair) which was a dramatic documentary for the Malta University radio. This latter work, on Mary Magdalene, mixes mysticism with realism and sensuality in a poetic way that garners cultural facts on this interesting woman.

In this introduction there is space only to talk in a general way about a few aspects of his poems.

Peresso's poetic orientation

Peresso's poetry encourages readers to scrutinize the language it uses for the understanding of the content and force of the poems. Much of his poetry turns the readers' attention to particular issues in human conduct, and therefore its ultimate aim is to lead the readers to think of themselves. The sparse details about the addressee seem to confirm this aim.

Among Peresso's methods of drawing readers into his poetic environment we find the displaying of private thoughts and the use of a familiar (conversational) tone. There is a certain confidentiality in these poems because very often they use the intimacy of a confessional mode assisted effectively by the use of the second person pronoun. Often there is no explicit "you"—the explicit addressee (even if it is non-human). *The Carob* seems to be an exception in this collection—and, furthermore, he uses a spoken style to let readers construct an implied addressee. Thus, in his poetic orientation there is a conative focus: he involves an orientation towards the addressee as we find in *Like a Book*. However, the second person often functions as an imaginary lover, as is quite evident from poems like *The Stilled Water of Your Eyes, A List, Tangible Dream, You are No Magdalene,* and *A Poem Written in a Park in Bruxelles.* But we must understand that his love in *Rational Love* is not physical. Sometimes first person and second person identities are merged showing that he holds his woman close to him inside his thoughts.

These poems include a shadowy presence of the second person.

The use of this second person causes the reader to identify more closely with the poem's theme. But at the same time I suspect that, in some of his writings, a

10

poem's narrative details belong to the poet himself, so that we can interpret the second person as another side of his personality. The mixture of first person and second person protagonists in a poem is really an instance of the poet talking to himself, which reminds us of Jacques Derrida's phrase *s'entendre parler* (i.e. to hear oneself speak) which makes the poet in both positions of sender and receiver in the poetic communication. Such poems may be taken as instances of interior monologues that expose the poet's psychology.

We can even assume that the use of the second person, at times, is a move to generalize recognition so as to lead the readers to distance themselves from any particular identification. These poetic experiences make us ready to interpret his language in terms relevant to humanity in general—a significant point in human relationships.

The aesthetic surface of Peresso's poems is rather smooth and clear, since rhythm, language, and lineation all work in combination for the general effect. In his compositions, he takes into account the theme (an area of inner thought) and the form (the external appearance of the poem) so that the two are conceivably in productive tension. One of the poems where we can find such a situation is *The City of the Knights* which taunts us into participating in the poem's action where we have to face the tension between the past and the present. However, in *Quiz Show* it is the form's terseness that creates the tension to depict contemporary emotional indifference in love.

On another occasion, we perceive in him an essential sense of existentialism that helps him build a relation with Christ to such an extent that he identifies himself with Christ's humanity in *Christ's Silent Soliloquy Before Herod,* a dramatic monologue which shows a consciousness that is in quest of a Christian elaborate meaning. Enunciating that there are "those whose smile / Is a dead breath of insincerity", he announces himself an individual thinker looking at his times and finding refuge in poetry. This monologue is a recognition of the cleavage between traditional faith (or the established religion) and contemporary reason (or the current culture). These thoughts are aslo echoed briefly but effectivley in *When God is Silent.)*

Peresso's intellectual climate

The poems show the connection at work between the subjective interior (mostly the concept of self) and the objective exterior (including reality and culture). The self (which sometimes is given to us in direct snatches) acts as a controlling force that endeavours to evaluate cultural and moral constructs. Such a poetry is also bound into a dialogue with the various subjects of his allusions. For instance, we encounter art in Botticelli's "Birth of Venus" (*On the Shores of Your Lips*) and, with a sense of mystery, in Leonardo da Vinci's Mona Lisa (*To La Gioconda*) so that the poetic self enters into a process of dialogue with these artistic works, and we realize that his poetic utterances include collaboration with the aesthetic reality they present. He also incorporates, among others, biblical allusions (in *You are No Magdalene* and in *Christ's Silent Soliloquy Before Herod*), mythology (in *My Aphrodite* and in *Winter*), philosophy (in *Cogito, ergo sum)* and music (in *Those Who Inherit the Wind*).

Typical of him, too, are the subtle cultural remarks like when he says, "I walked into the chiaroscuro of my memories" (*A Poem on My Birthday*) where he uses an artistic term to depict the contrasting shades of his memories. Or when he says, "Your treasured seeds measure wealth in carats" (*The Carob*) which is an etymological reference to the fact that the word "carat" comes from an Arabic term that means carob seed. And the four elements of ancient philosophy are culturally "kneaded together in a loaf of bread" (*A Loaf of Bread*).

His dialogic technique is impregnated with meaning as his work generates the fundamental reality that a poem is not an isolated construct but a poetic interaction between ideas from other intellectual spheres. His cultural references combine grace and depth, showing how complex a force is his poetic urge.

His intellectual climate includes an intimate purpose when it comes to symbolism. Artistically, within his speculative thought the symbolic becomes true and active on the poetic plane of reality. Let me explain by looking at his attitude to the seasons which commonly correspond to the four stages of human life. Peresso uses personification to add on to this cycle. Winter is seen as "the bringer of life / —and death", greeting "the color-eyed / Glints of spring" (*Winter*); and spring is "the smile of a creative Poet", but it is also "a dead flower in the city" (*Spring*). Yet *'Tis Sad to Weep Alone in Spring*, for spring is "the interpreter/ Of your unuttered words". And at the beginning we are told that "Autumn is the elegy of summer", and then later we are informed that "Every leaf that falls" is seen as a "footprint of eternity" (*An Autumn Leaf*).

Focusing on "Autumn is the elegy of summer. / The fall of light" we realize that there are meanings to be discovered here. The juxtaposition of autumn and summer and the imagery of diminishing light stimulate the readers into a new sense of reality that relates to the physical condition of the poet—Peresso's eyesight is becoming poorer with age. This text is more than just a thought on the alternation of the seasons. The rhythm of human life contains the stages in the cycle of development from maturity to decline. "The fall of light" (cf. the fall of the Roman Empire or the Fall of man) sounds important and it is burdened with implications because symbolically and traditionally light is the manifestation of morality and of the intellect (e.g. people become illuminated). And the song of sorrow for the death of maturity can be taken figuratively (at times with a dose of cynicism) on the socio-political plane as a reference to recent and contemporary times full of terrorism, abuse, artificiality, drugs, holocaust etc. (*A List, Crepuscular Moments, The Women With No Hair*). In Peresso's poetic vision, light is man's creative force; and although on the personal level his summer is over, psychologically these poems show that he is becoming illuminated because he is aware that poetry is a source of light that gives him spiritual strength in his verbal expression.

To mention one example of his illuminated mind we can look at the anaphora in the short poem *The Women With No Hair*. The anaphora emphasizes the destruction of human individuality as humans act inhumanely towards humans. The anaphora and the nine short statements of the poem link it dialogically with the Beatitudes of the bible to create a contrast between inhumanity and blessedness; and the poem's conclusion might as well be that inhumanity is an albatross around history's neck.

The poet's self is, at times, presented in explicit snatches like when he says that he is the man who feels a stranger in his own dream (*Epilogue*) or that he knows he is a loser (*Hidden Thoughts*). And he tells us that he loves his woman in his mind (*Rational Love, I Cannot Love You More*)—here he presents an intellectual love—and that he lives in a world that spits "slogans snatched/ From an over-used Thesaurus of Nonsense" (*Crepuscular Moments*). These are snippets that eventually build a profile of a Platonic lover with emotional and psychological problems in an artificial or insincere environment. Yet implicitly his poetry tells us that his intellectual attitude is very fertile and fecund. He communicates not facts and learning but himself through his experience and his interpretation of cultural discernment. Furthermore, personal existence is viewed as a temporal process, and poems like *Epilogue, A Poem on My Birthday,* and *'Tis Sad to Weep Alone in Spring* include the passage of time in a subjective way.

Conclusion

In Ġorġ Peresso's free personality there is an intellectual attitude that argues a generosity of mind and spirit. His poetry is well crafted and packed with meaning not only in itself but also in being dialogic with other sources. The poems may be simple thoughts but they certainly generate moments of reflection and sometimes great concepts or sentiments. Thought in Peresso is relevant and pertinent to his existence.

- Charles Briffa

Biographical note of Charles Briffa

Professor Charles Briffa lectures on the theory and practice of translation and on Maltese literature at the University of Malta. He is actively involved in broadcasting literary and linguistic programs on the radio and on television. He is a member of the Poetics and Linguistics Association (UK). He wrote extensively, in both Maltese and English, on the stylistic qualities of Maltese literary works and has translated several works, compiled several dictionaries, and edited various works.

*Autumn is the elegy
of summer.*

The fall of light.

Tangible Dream

Your liquid smile
Mischievously stolen
From the rivers of heaven
Where willows never weep
And ripples run with angels,
Bemused my greyish dawn—
And kept me musing till the night
Engulfed me in the colors
Of this affresco, warm with the scent of blossom.

"It is a dream," I sighed
"only a dream, not tangible."
Indeed it was a dream came true. And tangible.

The Carob
(*Dedicated to an old Carob*)

The sturdy evergreen protecting tree,
An ancient emblem for all seasons,
With roots delving in the stubborn rocks
And spreading dominance underneath
the unknown soil.
Mellifluous libation for mythical gods
And fodder for the famished beasts.
Friend of the whimpish wind,
playmate of the gusty rain,
Insolent and rugged rival of the solar rays,
Indolent gazer at the chiaroscuro of the night.
Yet poised against the background of the sky
With venerable dignity of an unfallen giant.
Your treasured seeds measure wealth in carats
And string beads of ancient heavenly prayers…,

Tree of my Mediterranean generation,
Humble and great,
An undying god of yore,
Il-harruba, the carob.

This short poem was included in the documentary
"The Carob", concerning the carob trees in Malta.

Like a Book

I will unfold my body like a book
In front of you.
A book a body
Full of words and phrases
And paragraphs and chapters
And punctuations and all
My exclamation and question marks
And dotted full stops and twisted commas
All my metaphors and similes
My grammar and my syntax
My footnotes and references
And Capital Letters and small letters
And photos black and white and sepia
And multi-colored pictures
And pencil-drawings
All my beliefs and doubts
All my naive and nonsense stories
And heavy thoughts
All my tears and laughter
My past and future.

I will unfold my body like a book
In front of you
Till THE END.

The Stirred Water of Your Eyes

I will carry you *vade mecum*
On the shelves of my mind,
And write you a poem on the palm of my hand
To remember it on misty voyages.
Your words flow streams in my veins
And your steps are waves approaching
In the trembling silence of the night
With the fragrance of the sea.
Like an old helpless psalter
I will hang my olive-colored lyre
Filled with clear metaphors and hidden love,
On the dripping branches of unsung desires,
Waiting for the winged messenger
To move in spirals
The blue-eyed waters of the dormant pools.

And then I rest in the stirred up water of your eyes,
In the shade of the arches of your arms.

PostScript: The metaphors of this poem are largely inspired by the story told by John Ch. 5 about a pool in Bethzatha (perhaps meaning The city of the Olives or Oil) where people met to be cured when the angels of the Lord stirred up the water. In Maltese, Oil is ZEJT, Very similar ZATHA.

Vade mecum is a Latin phrase describing a manual, book, with useful hints and directions

A List

I hate a lot of things.
This is a random sample
For your perusal.

I hate waiting in interminable queues.
I hate waiting at the bus stops.
I hate missing the bus by just a second.
I hate filling questionnaires
　　And paying surcharged bills.
I hate half-baked bread and half-baked ideas.
I hate fast-food and slow-moving Work in Progress.
I hate being taken for a ride by pompous politicians.
I hate platitudes and hate-fomented-articles.
I hate wars and victories after wars.
I hate the depravity of those who steal
Hues and perfumes from the valleys,
And the innocence of a tree and of a smile.
I hate the felling of old houses with
Memories and pictures on the dying walls.
I hate the smell of pollution in my breath,
Humidity traveling down my bones
And the slurping mud hindering my pace.
I hate the fetid smell of drooping lassitude
And the smell of boredom.
I hate dreamless nights and days
wandering in amnesia.
I hate myself when I am petulant and vain,

And….and…

I hate unending Sunday sermons
Whirling like draughts from
a broken stained-glass window
Around my confusion and my conflicts,
I hate withered flowers and burned garlic,
I hate an empty paper and an empty mind,
I hate looking in vain for a book on my shelves,
I hate listening to the news promising
Heaven and Hell,
I hate waiting in gray corridors of power,
I hate kissing bums.

But I don't hate waiting for you
And I love kissing you—
For I love you.

You are no Magdalene

You are no Magdalene
Shedding seven skins of seven devils
Unveiling the perfume of your hidden treasures.
And I am no Christ,
Redeemer and healer,
Waiting for the balsam and the oil
To be poured on the dust of my bare feet.
Your oil burns my hidden wounds,
More than five wounds,
Into flames dancing with the darkness of the cave
And the river in my veins
While your hands caress my body
For the last sunset
In the horizon of my dying wants.
Your veils like wild flowers in the untrodden path
Mark the garden of my last breath.

And the empty tomb
Calm like a silent sentinel
Awaits the setting of the night.

I am no Christ
You are no Magdalene.
Don't wait in vain for the gardener
To indicate the empty tomb.
Just keep me in your heart
Like a wild flower at the end of the untrodden path.

My Aphrodite

There is a distant bay in Paphos where rugged rocks
Like pillars of raving ancient temple
Scrape the sky for unheard choruses
    in crosswinds' harmonies
Like waves –warm waves - in full red robes
Stolen from the cheeks of the horizon
And the glints of a red orange.

The rising sun is as wide as the sea,
The waves bring pentagrams of joyful sighs
And then an ode of asymmetrical dimensions
Rises from the unknown fathom—
Darkness when kissed by the rays of sun
Turns in blown white and lips of colored brilliance
Catch the fragrance of the air.

And there comes She,
    the deity of my winged and restless mind,
In a lingerie of salted myth.
And there her birth renewed,
    disclosed like a pearl in a vaulted shell,
Every time I think of her,
My Aphrodite.

Paphos is considered to be the place in Cyprus where, according
the Greek myth, Aphrodite, the goddess of love, was born from the
waves.

A poem written in a park in Bruxelles
During the South Africa World Football Cup

With a swarm of vuvuzelas in the background
And strolling geese trumpeting their
presence in the park
While a swan dances with the clouds
I strive to write you a poem,
But my thoughts and metaphors
Fall helpless like
Dry weeping-willows.

For today please accept
A pre-programmed phrase
Chosen from the manual of Easy Useful Words:
I love you.
Tomorrow
I will tell you how much
And show you how.

Those Who Inherit the Wind

(An extract from the novel Those Who Inherit the Wind. *It evolves around a defrocked priest because of his out-spoken ideas against the Church in the religious-politcal crises in the early thirties of the last century. He prefers a self-imposed exile in France where he becames a known author under a nome-de-plume. He returns back for a short while in the late fifties to find Malta going through another similar crises. He meets a young unmarried woman, pregnant, who is fond with every thing that is Frenxh. He reads to her, against the bakcgroubd of Kustz's nysuc, an extract for his French novel. This selection is transalted by Elisabeth Fenech and the author.)*

He put on the record-player. Together with Marija, he listened to Liszt's *Benedction de Dieu dans la solitude.* He remained silent, then uttering slowly a selection from the poem by Lamertine:

D'où mei vien, ô mon Dieu!Cette paix qui m'inonde?

"Marija, this is not a quesion put by someone who doubts, let alone by someone who does not know, but by someone who is mesmerized. There are only two ways to express this feeling of astonishment: by silence and by a question."

Then he stopped for a while, leaving the music embracing them, the piano spreading the meaning which words are unable to express. Marija couldn't resist looking at him, with his eyes downcast as if he were praying not just listening. "This strange man is an extraordianry man," thought Marija. Then he talked again, his profound voice mingling with the mytserious piano music.

"The extrovert Liszt, the virtuosist Liszt, the braggart Liszt, the restless Liszt, with this kind of music, taming himself and turning himself into a mystiic.

Mesmerized and humble. The true Liszt...different from that of the hectic Rhapsodies, sensous with gypsy blood runing in his veins. A complete kind of music different from the famous *Etude,* well known for their demanding techinque. Even from the music *de Pèlerinage* included in his three volumes connected with his visits, like a tourist and a pilgrim, across Switzerland of the Alps and legends, through Italy of writers and painters and unique cities, especially Florence, and Rome of the strident morning church bells, and the enchanting sound of the fountains and the wind in the trees of Villa Tivoli, where the old *abbé* used to hide after one of his many love affairs...He was deeply loved and pampered and seduced by different women even in his old age."

Anton smiled for a while, a condescending smile, then continued. "The sinner and the penitent Liszt...His dualistic and contradictory yet fascinating aspects of his life are all included in this collection of *Harmonie poétique et Réligieuses,* especially those compostions inspired by poems of Lamertine...He managed to turn music into a liturgy of thought...Here is the true Liszt, the interior pilgrim praying and meditating immersed in the notes of music. Trying to find himself with the question *Que veux-je? What do I want?* Truly, a question which is full to the brim with dynamism, so a question of those who never stop searching. In this music to which we are listening, Marija, don't try to capture the music of a tourist fascinated by the landscape and the culture of Europe. This is the voyage of the soul. But having said that, I must admit that the music composed for *Hamonies* is rather eclectic and not perfectly unified. Each number reflects different moments of his numerous crises as a lover and a sinner. "But there are half a dozen especially the one we are listening to, *Benediction de Dieu dans la solitude*, that are a mystical work of genius rather than just music. How can it be that Liszt, a composer of music such as this, did not go to heaven, if heaven exists, despite the turbulence in his life. Artists without a troubled life, are really few. Art is above and beyond a measured existence, correct behaviour and wisdom of man. God only knows what he created when he let artists, composers, painters, sculptors, authors, become his own image, like gods. I know, I am falling into Pantheism like Lamartine and Liszt. I've gone on too much, haven't I? When I start talking about Liszt, I find it difficult to curb this temptation. Liszt in a way is a temptation...Shall I say, thank God?"

"It's fine, it's fine. You've fascinated me, believe me." Her voice was an outburst of sincerity.

And they kept on listening to the notes softening up to the last beats. Both of them, Marija and him, sitting at the edge of the bed.

"You were going to read me another passage before I stopped you."

She found it quickly. Towards the end.

"This," She almost insisted.

Anton gazed at the page.

"My favorite," he said and added, "When the pilgrim visits chapels in medieval villages spread out in the Beaujolais region, specifically in the *Pays des pierre doree'*, where the limestone with which the chapels, the houses and chateaux are built take on a golden hue like honey."

A short silent breath. Then he started reading.

"The pilgrim was wrapped by the chiaroscuro of the old church, part of a castle that faced and included the village of Oingt with all its history. A mysterious light, blended with the golden dark stone, came through the

colored glass. His eyes rose up towards the abside, held in place by eight half arches, resembling Carthusian monks, with their heads covered, praying. Eight, as much as the eight beatitudes guiding the terrestrial church towards its journey to Heaven...wherever it may be. And his silence was a thought, his thought a prayer.

He went out of the church, looming high but without pride, protected like a castle but welcoming. Its stone, which is used in the village buildings, such as the many houses leaning into each other, and embedded into the narrow, winding streets, the castles and watchtowers, is of a golden hue or washed in dark honey. He touched the wall. The old stone is alive and delicate as if he is touching an icon or an old relic.

The view from the hill, spread out before him as far as the eye could see, brought him a scene of sleepy, sensual hills resting side by side. And expanses of vineyards, one after another, straight as hermits walking into prayer. The vineyards were heavy with grapes, their juices teased by the rays of the sun. He was aching for that vision and the smell of the fields where he was brought up. Even for the few vineyards of his father. And for his mother and father. He tried to remember a few words from the poem by Lamartine, 'Les Morts'.

'Ils ont aussi passé sur cette terre...

Oui sont-ils? Qui nous le dire?

Heureux les morts qui meurent dans le Seigneur!'

But at that moment, the small ringing of the bell from the belfry shocked him out of his thoughts blending with death. The evening Ave Maria rang. Its sound echoed throughout. The first weak tones reminded him of the first notes, resembling a small bell, with which Liszt opens his Maria, in imitation of that bell's salute. He had heard that Ave Maria at a concert in Paris and the notes of that piece of music together with other musical pieces by Liszt became embedded into him like a musical background accompanying all his thoughts. Even his silences.

He went down the stairs in front of the church and passed through the streets still treasuring voices and sounds of wounding and fighting and victory and loss. He became saddened, in the way those who know history and silence are saddened, and he escaped, sauntering, towards the vineyards until the bells of the chapels beautifying the hills could not be heard anymore. Until the music that he carried within him no longer echoed inside him. He needed silence after that experience. He needed to be alone, he needed solitude, smelling the perfume of the insatiable vineyards, dissolving in the air."

Oralities

*(A poem written for a conference
at Orense about Oralities.)*

On the shores of your lips
Arrive the waves of sounds and thoughts
Born silently in the labyrinth of your mind—
Your first cry with shining eyes
On the dawn of the first light;
Your mumbled "mamma",
The building of your stark vocabulary;
Your sighs and cries
And rhymed magical prayers,
Spells of your desires,
Entwined with nonsense
So that God may understand them;
And legends and proverbs
Filled with dug-out wisdom,
From the dark depth of time;
And hymns of joy and glory and languid sadness.
And songs with glints of foolish merriment.

On these shores lies, like a naked Venus,
In a lingerie of salted myth,
(O Formosa dies!) the past when words
Were born and stories molded.

'Tis Sad to Weep Alone in the Spring.

When nothing is left but your silence
Shuddered by perfumed breeze,
'Tis sad to weep alone in spring.
Each blossom is a chant,
Each flower is a song.
In spring.

When nothing is left but your thoughts
Scattered like taunted leaves,
'Tis sad to walk alone in spring.
Each swallow is a dance.
Each robin is a dawn.
In spring.

When nothing is left but your past
Confused by tortured scores
'Tis sad to dream alone in spring.
Each color is a smile.
Each sunset is a muse.
In spring.

Let spring be the interpreter
Of your unuttered words.

Till autumn.

Face

It is a face of a woman,
the face of the woman I love,
the face of the land
after the first rain.
The land I love.

Hidden Thoughts

Your eyes are the profile of your hidden thoughts,
Blurred and misty,
Ebbing remote shores of vague desires.
I dare not ask
What lies beyond your liquid eyes.
I am afraid to ask.
Each answer holds more questions.
I do not haggle with your gaze.
I know I am the loser.
I simply gaze and remain silent
Listening to the sigh of hidden thoughts.
And vague desires.

Crepuscular Moments

This sunset
Clad in purple robes and satin smiles
Stolen from forgotten oriental fables,
Bemuses my untuned heart.
I must admit, I had a good dinner
And a glass of chilled Chenin Blanc.

But as an unwanted guest
The anchor man was reading
With personalized passion
The Evening News.
The same old stories. Never changing.
War. Attacks, Rape. Terrorism.
Drugs and overdose. Crises.
Hurricanes with gentle names of women
And the ferocity of Furies,
Hauling vengeance bleeding havoc.
A terrorist claiming Paradise
With an unleashed blood bleeding dagger
In the name of a god gnawing
Bodies freshly killed.
And rockets, pointed vengeance,
 Penetrate the shaken sky
And disturb the waves in open seas.
Children stolen of their flowering innocence,
And their right to play and laugh.
And smile even mischievously.

Their eyes imploring silently, albeit accusing,
A land, a house. Food and water
That taste of perfumed soil
And of the first rain revived.
And politicians, with a face of steel,
Spit their slogans snatched
From an over-used Thesaurus of Nonsense.

Anguish disturbed the amber light in my eyes.
I turned in anger.
Unplugged my mind.
Preferred a glass of chilled Chenin Blanc in my hand
Gazing at the vesper of the day.
And your silhouette
Against the light
Of the fading crepuscular scene.
Lest I felt guilty.

All horizons are illusions.

ঔ৯ঔ৯

5) Writing a poem
Is like losing your path in a wood.
And you become a flower, a shrub, a tree,
A brook, a spring, a rock,
A bird, an animal.
Wild and gentle.
Afraid and mesmerized.
You cannot write a poem
Unless you are wild and gentle
Afraid and mesmerized
Lost in a wood.

ঔ৯ঔ৯

6) the stained glass of my thoughts
Worship the wonder
Cowed in silence.

ঔ৯ঔ৯

7) We cry when we are born
And joy and life fill our lungs.
But we die in silence,
The last breath and sigh
Leaving out without a word our dark lungs.
That is why death is a cruel finale.

Because we are not allowed to cry.
If only we could cry when we are dying!

ৡৡৡৡ

8) A poem is the encounter
Of my colors with your eyes.

ৡৡৡৡ

9) Inside me I carry you,
An unborn cry.

ৡৡৡৡ

10) The dry silence
Is stretching its arms
Around the unmapped desert
I fear to pace. In darkness.
Only the vagrant owl
 With outstretched silence and moon-eyed gaze
Finds pleasure
In the darkness of this bleak domain.
And back to home.
Without giving a hoot.

The Wounded Field

I am a wounded field.
The seeds spread on it
Like salt on open wounds,
Stun the dry weak soil.
But if one day on this wounded field
A wild flower grows,
Leave it there in the middle of the wounded field,
Come and watch it till it dries
Because you are the only one
Capable of understanding and explaining
What a wild flower has to tell
On the wounded field.

To La Gioconda

On the twilight of your lips
There are no landscapes,
supine, shrouded
In misty silhouettes.
And melodies never sung.
Words drown like an ochre sun
In archaic myths
On the shores of your poignant forehead.
The teasing silence watches
From your eyes, questioning
My intrusive eyes
Trying to find in you, staring at me,
Rippling discomfort,
Someone I know. Or knew.
Perhaps myself.
I'm sure, I have seen you before.
Envisaged your smile—
enclosing words and silence,
While I drifted away on barren fields
Without a shadow.

Leonardo, for sure,
Painted a question.
Not just a face with dried-out smile
With autumn leaf between the lips.

At Times

At times
The Mediterranean
Is like a page from a novel
With words smelling of salt and sea.
Inside its phrases
metaphors and images glimmering
Open as the horizon.
And dreams. And hopes

At times.

At times,
The Mediterranean
Is a novel with pages fluttering in a gale
Pages which become the crests of waves
In which the perfumed words drown,
As do the glimmering phrases
metaphors and images
as wide as the horizon.
And dreams. And hopes

At times.

(Translated by Irene Mangion from the libretto for a cycle of three operas Belt Il-Bniedem (City of Humanity).

Christ's Silent Soliloquy Before Herod.

O please, stop jabbering Herod, you Tetrarch,
In front of me in a Greek Mask,
Belching nonsense as you strut
With fallen dignity the power of your empty mind.
I had a long hard night at Caiphas's den.
They spit accusations on my face
Till the cock crowed to claim his space.
And then at Pilate's hall
Accused and scorned,
With thorns to crown my head,
A dirty rag on my flogged shoulders,
And shouts of "Crucify this criminal,"
Shredding my innocence,
While justice was condemned in the praetorium.
He was confused, the Governor,
With seven wrinkled doubts
Etched on his forehead,
To hand me like an unstained lamb
To quench the ritual of a feverish mob.
He sent me here before you
Tetrarch; you, beheader of my Prophet
Whose head still hounds your turgid dreams.
You turned your body into a den of vice.
Where harlots don't disdain to price their spell.
An unveiled body haunts your crown,
A man of no avail, dressed as a clown.

You are worth less, Herod, You Tetrarch.
Than a fish-smelling shekel paid in temple tax.
And you don't even match the price
For two quivering sparrows
Sold for a denarius at the temple market,
While the poor young widow's tin coin offering,

Her humble homage towards the Rock of God
Is gold in my Celestial Court.
And all your gold is just a hoard of rusted iron.
Your strident voice resounds the smell of hell
While it was heaven the untuned sound of flute
Played by a boy near the temple Gate
While I was carried here for your delight.
Your eyes two nests of moulting hawks,
Have never sought my eyes. Perhaps afraid
To see in them my Prophet crying
"Behold the Lamb of God,"
And the amazed water of Jordan,
Witness to a Voice proclaiming me The Son,
Still sings my praise.
While a chorus of reeds restless as a psalm.
But you are deaf like an abandoned tower,
Flaunting the standard of an impotent power.

Do you expect a one-man show today,
You Tetrarch, Herod,
The spiting image of a fox,
To entertain your odd curiosity
And give some fun to those whose smile

Is a dead breath of insincerity?
I will not exhibit my powers from above
To serve your drunken thoughts.
Keep to yourself the scorn of your applause.
Keep to yourself your serpent wine with poison.
For all the clusters of Canaan grapes
Fermenting in your cellars,
I will not fill your jars with the best wine
As I once did in Cana in a wedding feast.
Or kindle light on darkened eyes,
And play with words on slurring tongues,
And restore strength to crippled, the infirm.
I have no time to waste on idiots
and their every whim.

Your futile speech, still lingers on,
You barren land, where evil spirits dwell
And swine with jewelled teeth munch acrid pods.
Utter your stark command
 With pompous grin:
"Clad him in white this mad hallucinator.
Escort him back to Pilate
With pipers out of tune
And drummers out of time."
You, Tetrarch, Herod,
The smell of sweat, and perfume and of sin
Lies like a torpid beast in this cheap inn.

It's almost noon and the impatient death
Is keeping guard on the cross-hole of Calvary,

The cross will be my cradle for my death,
And Mother's eyes two lullabies
To fondle me toward Eternal Life.
I crave for that: The Cross and Mother's love
Roll down your cartouche monologue,
Cut short your foul verbosity
And send me back to Pilate.
He has the right to sign my final hour
And not a sullen fool like you.
At last, the undeciphered prophecies will unfold
While my nailed body grasps for breath
On Calvary. And darkness falls.
The prologue of the Light.
So send me back to Pilate.
History like unleashed wind,
 Awaits the end of your anaemic speech.
Don't steel my Time. Don't curb my day.
You are intruder in this Passion Play.

My hour has arrived. As prophesised.
The long shadow of time approaches Calvary.
The sixth and the ninth hours
Clad in darkness, wait for me outside the walls
 And death heralds its greatest moment of all times.
I crave to say the final words: All things are done.
So now it's time to close your greedy snout.
You sickened me, you clown, you blabbermouth.

Entertaining Dreams

The reed was still young
And the tune was still wet
When I tried to embrace you with a song
To entertain my dreams.
And the sound of the sea deep as a chant
Engulfed my new bewilderment
Which I retained from my lost childhood.
To entertain my dreams.

Now that the reed is dry and cracked
And the tune is breathless
And the chant of the sea has lost its salt
I still see you dancing between each verse
And hiding behind words, and teasing me
From one stanza to another,
As we used to play in our weaved childhood.

Trying till the end
To entertain my dreams.

৵৵৵৵

An Autumn Leaf

Every leaf that falls
Weary with feeble colors
Like music in *diminuendo*
Denudes the skeleton of life
And the arcane sigh
Of a God that plays Hide and Seek
In the Garden of Wonder.

Every leaf that falls
Evokes the rustle of the passing time,
Every leaf that falls
Has the footprint of eternity.

৵৵৵৵

Winter

Winter the bringer of life
—and death—
On thunderous wings,
And dreams that melt with rain
To fertilize the soil.
Sensuous and passionate god.

Zeus of all the seasons,
Dominant and vociferous,
Huffing bull from a roaring distance,
Disguised seducer and rapist
Of fruit-scented virgins.
And budding flowers with groping hands.
The red robe of the horizon
Heralds, with teasing breeze,
At last, the end
Of your stumping gasps.

And the hibiscus,
Swan flower,
In flimsy crimson satin dress,
Emits the last perfumed breath.
To greet the color-eyed
Glints of spring.

৵৵৵৵

Spring

Captives of dawn
Step out barefooted
With ritual dance of yearning freedom
Kissing with their eyes the breathing land.
Life comes to concert on this stage
Performing an orchestrated partiture.
Spring, the smile of a creative Poet,

Playful child and divine Psalter
Takes center stage.

That was in the beginning.
That how it was meant to be.

Then man created cities
With roots of steel
That smothered and killed spring.
Spring is a death flower in the city.

ഉ൫ഉ൫

Midsummer's Night's Dream

Eyelids
Dozing in a wood
Of fragrant colors
In this no extinguishable summer.

ഉ൫ഉ൫

51

A Loaf of Bread

The golden shovels of wheat
Are treasures which the soil shares.
With our tired body and spirit.
The four elements—fire, air, water, and earth—
Are kneaded together in a loaf of bread
And its fragrance is our breath and strength.

The City of the Knights

In the City
Where with dignified and steady dominance
Stalked and strolled the black-cloaked Knights
In the imposing shadows
Of Churches, Palaces, and Auberges,
Filled with rays of glory and chiaroscuro of awe,
We walked this evening
Embracing our unuttered feelings
As the Fortifications of our City
Embody it with pride.

In front of us the restless sea,
Swaying history on its crest.
And the curtsey
 Of the crimson and emerald horizon,
Above us the teasing clouds
Like children in a court-yard.
And our dreams.
In front of me, you.
And the humming blue of your eyes.
Inside me, your voice. And you.
On me the perfume of your body
Like an orchard
like the waves
In the City of the Knights.

This evening

It seems that the Knights
Had build this City
Just for us.
For us they built the walls
To hide and guard our impatient eyes.

In the chiaroscuro of this city,
Perhaps tonight
Two foregone lovers
From the pages of an unwritten romance,
He cloaked in black
and the eight-pointed cross,
she dressed with passion of the humble,
Have joined our enamoured hiding place
Within the City of the Knights,
The city of lost lovers.

The Last Wave

The wave this evening, in moon color,
Tired but relaxed on the still sand.
My scattered thoughts,
Reluctant clouds without direction,
Speechless forms,
On the sleepy wave, tired and relaxed.
The last wave, in moon color,
Our love, wave musing with the moon.

Rational Love

I cannot carry you in my heart.
The arteries are blocked.
The atria and the ventricles are closed.
The chambers not available.
But...
I'll carry you in my mind.
I am an open-minded man!

The Women With No Hair

The women with no hair.
Their bones hanger for shriveled skin,
One face, one sigh, one sadness, one house.
No address.
One breath. One death.
The women of Auschwitz.

Quiz Show

Do you love me?
The answer after the commercial break.

When God is Silent

Drop
By
Drop
Silence
Drips
Into the depths
Of Jacob's well.
God of Abraham, God of Isaac, and God of Jacob
Is silent
Silent
Silent.
Maybe he wept silently
And we did not hear Him.
Maybe silence
Drop
By
Drop
Is the sound
Of God's tears.

(Translated by Lydia Zammit.)

When

I am a blind man
When I walk alone,
I don't see clouds and the clear sky,
Flowers and trees and streams,
and birds and cars,
And dawns and sunsets,
and your blue eyes
when I walk alone.

And then in just one blink
I see the clouds and the clear sky,
Flowers and trees and streams,
And birds and cars,
And dawns and sunsets,
And your blue eyes.
When you walk with me.

When the sea

When the sea talks to you
Hush and stay still.
Let it roll, ripple, sway,
Flow, ebb.
It speaks to you.
Only he can let you know
What he heard over the horizon.

(Translated by Lydia Zammit.)

Serenade

A breeze rustles through the fronds
Making love with silence
and frolics with the flowers
which autumn had sheltered for her.
The greatest affection lies hidden.

(Translated by Lydia Zammit.)

Cogito, ergo sum

I am a script without an author.
I am a song without a singer.
I am a play without a stage.
I am a pilgrim without a sanctuary.
I am my own dream.
I am fragments of my illusions.
I think, therefore I am.
I exist. I think.

(Cogito, ergo sum, R. Descartes' axiom: I think, therefore I am.)

A Graphic Will on the Wall.

When on distant nights
　　Screams like prayers flickered the dask
And whips on bare bodies,
　　Denuded of their distressed illusions,
Struggled with the muscles of the hallowed bells,
　　I was still an unborn child of the stranded moon,
　　Playing on my own hide and seek
　　in the colorless dunes.

　　Then moon after moon and spheres after spheres
　　I came face to face with your last
Dry, silenced, fractured will
On the dry, silenced, fractured wall.
　.

　　When your furrowed lips cuddled the dust
Of an ancient spell like a still-born baby
Your grained hand scribbled
　　A cryptic message
On the cryptic wall that bore you to your death
Smelling of wild herbs like your ancient breath.

Only God understands the will of a dying witch,
The dying wish of a deadly wrench,
But God and fortune were looking somewhere else
When the dying fortune teller
Hushed her last Amen.

Her oral will unsure of sense
    is now an obscure epitaph
On the wrinkled wall.
While tourists, guided,
Pass by unaware of her last spell.

And the voice of the Tourist Guide goes on:
"On your left...on your right.
Look here, see that, watch this.
St. Angelo...St. Lawrence.
Souvenir shop....Lunch soon.
But of course, Madam,
if you don't like our local food
You can have fish and chips with HP sauce...
And for you, Sir, hamburger with BBQ sauce.
Follow me, please...left...right.
Here...this...that.
And the voice goes on.

A Poem on my Birthday

The early morning
was still breathing
the wet smell of the night,
and the dew, still relaxed
like a sleeping fairy in the pages my childhood.
And every thing was still,
even the wind and the leaves,
and the reluctant waves
when I walked into the chiaroscuro of my memories
to fetch a lost toy of my childhood.
And felt too old to walk for long,
too old to long for decayed images of the past.
But still too young to thrust myself
into the unknown ambers of the fretting dawns.
Today I rest and I stay still
like the wet smell of the night
and the relaxed dew
and the wind and the leaves and the waves.
Tomorrow is another day, they say.

Epilogue

…And the breeze
Flowing seven veils
In front of my eyes perfumed with the sea
Was dancing, eternal breath of youth,
On the excited cobbles.
And the wide-eyed shrubs looked by.
And the colored fishing boats, in their sleep,
Yawned to the teasing waves.
Only the seagulls, clad in candid defiance,
Tried to steel the scene.
For a while, I felt a stranger in my own dream,
Intruder on my own water-colored desires—
Till you came by, with the sound of your smile,
Echoing verses of poems I never wrote,
As if I knew you many, many dreams ago,
And moved my shriveled thoughts.

It was an epilogue.

NOTES

68